S0-ABF-308

A
Victorian
Teatime
Treasury

Angela Hynes

A Victorian Teatime Treasury

Angela Hynes

BOOKS 2000

Copyright c 1991 by
Angela Hynes

First Printing 1991
Printed in the United States
of America

**Library of Congress
Cataloging in Publication Data**

Hynes, Angela
A Victorian Teatime Treasury

Includes Index
1. Victoriana 2. Tea 3.
Entertaining

ISBN 1-879577-01-1

All rights reserved. No part of
this publication may be repro-
duced, stored in a retrieval sys-
tem, or transmitted, in any form
or by any means, electronic, me-
chanical, photocopying, re-
cording, or otherwise, without
prior written permission of the
publisher.

Notice: The information con-
tained in this book is true and
complete to the best of our
knowledge. All recommenda-
tions are made without any
guarantees on the part of the
author or Books 2000. The author and publisher disclaim all
liability in connection with the
use of this information.

Credits

Cover Photography/Jimmy Hynes

Cover Design/Kathleen Dantini

Cover Food Styling/Angela Hynes

"There are few hours in life more agreeable than the hour dedicated to the ceremony known as afternoon tea."

HENRY JAMES

(1843-1916)

Contents

PART ONE

An Invitation to Tea

You are graciously invited to tea. Come around 3:30p.m., and come hungry. The table will be laden with a selection of tasty little sandwiches, fluffy currant scones and strawberry preserves to spread on them, snappy ginger cookies, a pear tart, a lemon sponge cake, and jewel-colored bonbons. Of course there will be lashings of aromatic, steaming tea: perhaps robust Assam or classic Darjeeling.

But this is not just any afternoon tea. We are draping the table with grandma's damask cloth and lace doilies, setting out our best tea service or our charming collection of mismatched cups and plates, lighting a crackling fire, and filling the room with candles and flowers and ferns and keepsakes. We are taking a vacation from our technological and minimilistic age and luxuriating for a few hours in an engaging mix of sensuality and sentimentality. Because this is a recreated Victorian tea.

The Victorian age is more than just the period of time that loosely corresponds with the 1837-to-1901 reign of Queen Victoria, Britain's longest ruling monarch. The era encompasses a way of life, values, beliefs, and behaviors that, although long gone, have taken on a provocative appeal to those of us battling the rigors of daily existence in the late twentieth century. Entertaining Victorian style provides us an opportunity to escape for a while to a life of opulence and romanticism. By blending the best from the past with today's reality, we can add a little grace and civility to our existences.

The Victorians viewed entertaining at home as one of their more delightful recreations, and they hosted a good many leisurely luncheons and grand banquets that could last for up to three hours. But more than anything, the nineteenth century woman loved to attend and hold afternoon teas, both formal and informal.

Table Talk, a fashionable ladies magazine of 1893, described what we might call a casual get together. "An informal tea-sipping is nothing more nor less than a day 'at home' of a chosen friend. She stipulates an hour, usually between four and six of an afternoon, on her 'set-apart' day, and her *intimes* congregate to discuss tea and matters in general, in their most stylish toilets and becoming millinery."

The hostess would alert friends to her "set-apart" day by sending out a card one week before. It would likely read:

Mrs. George Morris Brown
At home from 3 until 5
Wednesday, Feb. 15, 1893

Guests would leave a calling card in a basket or on a tray in the hall, so that the hostess would know to whom she owed return visits. For a modern day adaptation of this practice, you might consider setting out a guest book for visitors to sign.

The same publication goes on to describe how the perfect hostess should comport herself. "In a corner of her drawing-room or parlor, whichever she prefers to entertain in, she sets a small table, daintily furnished with four to half-a-dozen cups and saucers, together with the kettle, the pot and required paraphernalia. Her pretty tea-gown envinces her taste in dress, while the snowy lace that falls back in rivalry from her white wrists as she pours the fragrant tea accentuates her profound regard for the aesthetic."

All of this, quite obviously, applies to the upper- classes. The Victorian era also saw the emergence of a middle-class that emulated the style of its betters, although having to make do with less. Henry Mayhew, in his 1851 book "London Labour and the London Poor," quotes a muffin man who sold his wares in the streets, probably mainly to these Victorian yuppies. "I turns out with muffins and crumpets, sir, in October, and continues until it get well into the spring. I sells a genteel thing. I like wet days best, 'cause there's werry respectable ladies what don't keep a servant, and they buys to save themselves going out. We're a great conwenience to the ladies...to them as likes a slap-up tea."

Victorian society was quite polarized with a huge poverty-stricken underclass that was so vividly brought to life by Charles Dickens. They, too, took tea although on a different scale. "Tea" was more likely to be the evening meal taken about six o'clock when the men came home from the factories or fields. It might consist of cold boiled beef or ham and potatoes; or a bowl of soup, bread and cheese, and plum pudding. All satisfying and hearty fare, often enjoyed before a blazing fire.

A Party for All Seasons

Any occasion was deemed appropriate for tea. Nursery teas, betrothal teas, picnic teas, amateur theatrical teas, holiday teas... all were popular.

For lavish affairs, *Table Talk* instructs the hostess to embellish her drawing-room this way. "Mantel banked with green foliage and la France rosebuds. Palms and cut flowers in bowls. Books of choice, engraving, photographs, etc., scattered about on corner tables. Table decoration, elegant in its simplicity. Cloth, white. Silver candelabra, many branched with perforated shades in pink. On one corner of the table, large cut-glass bowl filled with roses. At one end, tea service in silver." Clearly the Victorian definition of "simplicity" was a little different from our own.

Silver was one choice for tea equipage, but in well-to-do homes you were as likely to find teapots made from bone china or Sevres porcelain. Victorians of more modest means favored earthenware or lustreware. But in all cases the designs were elaborate and pots had complicated handles and spouts, and in some instances stood on little feet. Food was served on platters and in chaffing dishes. Cake stands, often with arched handles, were also popular. All came in china, crystal and sterling. Ceramics, pressed glass and silver plate again substituted when the real things were out of reach. Withy a little patience, all now can be found in antique shops, and will add to the ambiance of your tea.

Regardless of how humble the furnishings were, Victorians always arranged them beautifully and the food was extravagantly garnished. At dinner time, it was considered improper to have perfumed flowers on the table least the scent of the blossoms fought with the aroma of the food, and hostesses generally opted instead for elaborate epergns holding fruit and sweetmeats. But tea foods generally do not have strong odors, so fragrant flowers were considered more appropriate then. Roses were a perennial favorite, but Victorians also loved modest garden and woodland flowers such as sweetpeas, pansies, violets, and lily-of-the-valley. An anonymous verse written at the time and entitled "Afternoon Tea" sets the scene.

> *"The table was a pleasant sight*
>
> *With glass and china set;*
>
> *Upon it, roses, red and white*
>
> *Were mixed with mignonette."*

A cookbook of the period — "What to Serve and How to Prepare it at Afternoon Parties" — actually lists the appropriate floral decoration for each month: daisies in April, poppies in August, for instance. Often, a single blossom or a nosegay was presented to each guest.

Luscious Repasts

When it came to food, a Victorian tea was similar in many ways to the afternoon tea served today in hotels and tea rooms. Sandwiches, however, tended to be more elaborate. Often they were left open faced then rolled up and tied with tiny ribbons, or they were cut into shapes such as hearts and bells with cookie cutters.

The usual array of scones, cookies, tarts, and cakes was served. The Victorian era is especially interesting from a baking standpoint because it was during this period that kitchens began their evolution into those we are familiar with today. Open hearths gave way to ranges. Gas was first used for cooking in the 1860s, and electricity twenty year later.

The industrial revolution that transformed Britain and America also affected diet in other ways. The invention of the steamship enabled food to be brought from abroad without spoiling, and factory methods introduced the use of processed foods such as powdered chocolate and condensed milk.

Victorian cooks were enterprising in adapting old recipes that had been handed down through the ages, and in inventing new ones to take advantage of their innovative kitchen appliances. It truly was a golden age for baking.

New technology notwithstanding, a favorite pastime in winter months was toasting crumpets or tea buns at the open hearth. Spread with melting butter, honey or jam, they were a staple of an informal tea.

In summer, the Victorians invariably included a dessert item such as ice cream, sherbert or frappé on the tea menu. At any time of year, a dish of homemade sweetmeats or bon-bons was *de rigeure*. In deference to today's lighter tastes, I have substituted fruit on some of the menus in this book.

One item that brooks no substitution is tea, which, of course, is the mainstay of a tea party.

A Nice Cup of Tea

Tea has always been surrounded by a mythology that adds to its romance. The true beginnings of tea culture and the brewing of the plant's dried leaves into a soothing drink are lost in antiquity. But the most commonly held belief is that the plant originated in Northern India.

According to legend, a Buddhist monk called Daruma once nodded off while meditating. On awakening he was so enraged by his own weakness that he ripped off his eyelids and cast them on the ground. A tea bush sprang up where they fell. The astonished monk plucked some of the leaves, boiled them in water and drank the brew. He was so refreshed that he was able to continue his mediation.

The ancient Chinese also cultivated tea and celebrated it in their early written history. Chinese Buddhist monks introduced tea into Japan, where the preparation and drinking of tea developed into the ritual ceremony called Ch-No-Yu. The Japanese elevated the partaking of tea from a social pastime to an aesthetic cult. From Japan, tea spread to Java and the Dutch East Indies.

Tea was introduced to Europe in the 1600s by Portuguese merchants. Later, the Dutch formed the Dutch East India Company to import tea directly, and when the British realized how profitable a commodity it was, they too entered into the tea business.

At first, tea was the preserve of men in England. They drank it in coffee houses which were already established as excellent places to meet and make conversation. Then lovely, landscaped tea gardens serving women as well as men came into vogue. At Ranelagh and Vauxhall fashionable society would meet to see and be seen, and sip tea. As these tea gardens in turn lost popularity, tea-drinking became more of an at-home activity.

Legend has it that Anna, Duchess of Bedford, originated the fashion of afternoon tea. In the eighteenth century, servants started work before dawn to prepare big breakfasts for their masters. They had a few hours off in the middle of the day, so society ladies had a light,

makeshift lunch. Anna complained of a "sinking feeling" in late afternoon when there was still several hours to wait before dinner. She invited friends to share a cup of tea and an assortment of small sand-wiches and cakes in the afternoon when the maids came back on duty and could serve them.

By Victorian times the tradition of afternoon tea had become an important social event. Tea had a glamorous aura and the first China tea of the season brought exceptionally high prices on the London market. The tea was transported in clippers: fast, graceful sailing ships that could "clip" time from long ocean voyages. The crews of these ships were offered a premium per ton for the first tea to arrive in England. This lead to the exciting clipper races of the 1850s and '60s on which Victorian gentlemen wagered. The ships would leave Foochow during the dangerous south west monsoons, and often would arrive in London within hours of one another after over a hundred days at sea.

The burgeoning steam ship era and the opening of the Suez canal — always a hot topic of conversation at any Victorian gathering — put an end to the clipper. In any event, India was taking over from China as the world's most important producer of tea. A man named Robert Bruce discovered tea growing in the Brahmaputra river valley in the Assam province of India — then a British dominion — in 1823. By the time Victoria was made Empress of India in 1876, the Indian tea trade was well established and teas from Assam, Darjeeling and Nilgiri recog-nized as the best in the world, as they are today.

Pure black teas are the beverage of choice for the afternoon, and they come in a number of varieties. Some of the most superior are:

Darjeeling. Often called the "champagne of teas," Darjeeling is grown in the foothills of the Himalayas. It has a fine delicate flavor and a rich aroma some people find evocative of muscat grapes. If ever in doubt about which tea to serve, you cannot go wrong with this classic.

Assam. Assam is the largest single tea-producing area in the world. The tea grown there is full-bodied, pungent and malty. Hardened tea drinkers love it.

Nilgiri. Nilgiri teas are grown on the gentle slopes of the Blue Mountains in southern India. They have a light, mellow flavor. Less well-known to Americans than some other teas, it is beginning to make an impact on connoisseurs.

Ceylon. Tea grown in Sri Lanka (formerly Ceylon) is delicate and fragrant. The best comes from elevations over 4,000, so look for the words "high grown" on the package.

Tea blends are also acceptable fare for afternoon tea. By the far the most well-known is:

Earl Grey. This is a sweet, citrusy black tea flavored with bergamot. It is a favorite with those people who like to drink tea without milk or lemon.

In recent years black teas flavored with natural fruit oils, flowers and spices have appeared on the market. There is everything from Mandarin to peach, from blackberry to lemon, mango, pineapple, cinnamon, ginger, vanilla and brandy. Producing a slightly lighter drink than pure black teas, these fragrant brews go beautifully with the rich foods served at afternoon tea. And although not authentically Victorian, it is not hard to imagine how a nineteenth century hostess would have been enchanted by tea delicately infused with apricot or redolent of exotic cardamom.

There are any number of excellent brands of loose tea on the market (never use tea bags when entertaining). One brand in particular — Victoria's Treasure — fits the Victorian theme. The company imports gourmet teas directly from India and Sri Lanka, and its logo is an etching of Queen Victoria's monument in Calcutta. Tea is packaged in reusable wooden chests, brass caddies and unique, Indian clay pots, all of which are appropriate to keep on your table during tea to enhance the ambiance.

Once you have selected the tea of your choice, it is important to brew the tea correctly to bring out its full flavor. Follow this classic method:

- Fill your tea kettle with fresh, cold water.

- While waiting for the water to boil, rinse out your teapot with hot water and then wipe it dry. Heating the pot helps the flavor of the tea to "bloom."

- Put one teaspoon of loose tea in the pot for each cup of tea. Put the lid on the pot and allow it to stand until the water is boiled.

- When water has reached a full, rolling boil, take the pot to the kettle (so the water temperature does not drop by being off the heat too long), and gently pour the water over the tea leaves.

- Replace the lid on the teapot and allow the infusion to brew for three to five minutes, according to taste or the directions on the package. Stir once half way through the brewing time.

- Pour the tea through a strainer into cups and serve immediately.

- After pouring the first round, top up the pot with hot water.

For large tea parties — say, more than 20 guests — rent an urn from a party supply store so you can have a constant supply of boiling water with which to fill up your teapots. For a group of this size, you might considered having a choice of teas for your guests, perhaps a Darjeeling and a fruit flavored tea.

Offer your guests a sweetener and a choice of milk or lemon slices. Milk is traditionally taken with tea in England. The practice stems from the eighteenth century when people first started using delicate china cups and were afraid the hot tea would crack them. Incidentally, it should always be milk not cream, which is too rich for the delicate flavor of tea and does not mix well with the tannin. Adding lemon to tea is a Russian custom, and was introduced to England by one of Queen Victoria's daughters, who was married to the Emperor of Prussia.

Before proceeding with the menus for your Victorian tea, get properly in the mood by reading this essay written by Laura Coats Reed in 1894.

SHE POURS TEA

Dame Fashion waves her wand. Her gilded doors fly open. Within, the soft glow of many tinted tapers, and the hum of voices blended with the faint strains of mandolin and zithern. A prodigality of flowers, high carnival of bloom. Here, with winged petals spread, as though heaven itself were the ambition of its flight, an orchid. Anon, the fronded traceries of fern. Pervading all, the delicate perfume of each corolla's breath. Behold! Upon an ancient Heppelwhite, bedecked with snowiest, daintiest texture of the loom, the sovereign kettle is enthroned. Her subjects, ideal creations of ceramic art, await the royal bidding. From an illumed diaphanous conceit, comes a pale green shimmer. It falls upon a picture. Its frame, proud exotic. The face? You have seen it in a miniature. The coloring? It is found in a cameo. But stay! There is life within the Empire gown. The silken sea-green brocade rustles. A pair of dark brown eyes are gems that sparkle, luminous as a ray of sunset.

The head, poised like a blossom on its stem, bends with rhythm. The hand, adorned only with harmonious curves clasps the ivory handle of the tea pot. Ah, delightful pleasance! Bewitching embodiment of grace! A lovely girl pours tea!"

PART TWO

The Tea Menus

Valentine's Tea for Two

The true history of the romantic celebration on February 14th is lost in antiquity. That date is thought to be when early Christian martyr, Valantinus, was beheaded. On the eve of his death he wrote a farewell message to his jailor's daughter and signed it, "From your Valentine." The date also coincides with the ancient Roman festival in honor of the Goddess Juno. At this feast, young men drew, by lot, the names of the girls who were to be their partners at the celebration. Yet other experts believe the word Valentine is simply an adaptation of the Norman word "galatin," meaning gallant, or lover.

Whatever the origins, the tradition of exchanging gifts and cards was well established by the nineteenth century. The practice had great appeal to the sentimental Victorians. Early in the period cards were generally handmade and hand delivered. Later they were mass produced and mailed. Always they were elaborately made from lacy and embossed paper with painted hearts and flowers and sweetly polite messages in exquisite penmanship:

"Let soft love beaming from thine eyes

Speak rapture to my heart

And like the sun in eastern skies

Its cheering rays impart."

Victorians, of course, observed strict protocol in matters of courting. But today we can enjoy this romantic Valentine's tea for two without the benefit of a chaperone.

Menu for Two

Lobster Sandwiches

Devonshire Splits

Kissme Cake

Rose Water Cookies

Peppermint Creams

Victoria's Treasure Nilgiri Tea

Champagne (optional)

Lobster Sandwiches

Meat from a small lobster
2 hard-boiled egg yolks
2 tablespoons butter,
    melted and cooled
Salt to taste
1/2 teaspoon French
    mustard
4 slices fresh white bread
Parsley sprigs to garnish

≥ Pulverize lobster in a food processor or with a mortar and pestle. Add egg yolks and mash together. Moisten with melted butter. Season to taste with salt and mustard. Remove crusts from bread and spread two slices evenly with lobster mixture. Top with remaining bread slices. Cut each sandwich diagonally to make four triangles. Garnish with parsley sprigs.

Devonshire Splits

1 cup all-purpose flour
1-1/2 teaspoons baking
    powder
1/2 teaspoon baking soda
Pinch of salt
2 tablespoons butter,
    chilled and cubed
1 tablespoon sugar
1 egg, lightly beaten
1/3 cup of milk, if needed
Strawberry preserve
Heavy unsweetened
    whipped cream

≥ Preheat oven to 450F. Very lightly grease a baking sheet. Sift flour, baking powder, baking soda and salt together. Cut in butter until mixture is crumbly. Stir in sugar. Make a well in center of mixture; add egg and enough milk to make a dough that barely holds together. Turn out onto a floured board and knead lightly just until smooth. Roll out or pat dough to make a round about 3/4 inch thick. Cut in rounds with a 3-inch fluted cookie cutter. Arrange 2 inches apart on baking sheet. Brush tops lightly with milk. Bake 10 minutes or until well risen and golden. Transfer to a wire rack and cool 5 minutes. Split and serve warm, spread with preserves and a dollop of whipped cream.

Kissme Cake

🍂 Preheat oven to 350F. Grease a 9-inch cake pan at least 1-1/2 inches deep. Line bottom with wax paper. Bring 1 cup sugar, water and vanilla to boil. Remove from heat. Add half of both kinds of chocolate and stir until smooth. Break up butter into small pieces and whisk in half. Add remaining chocolate and butter. Thoroughly beat eggs with remaining sugar until pale yellow. Beat in melted chocolate mixture. Pour batter into pan. Place cake pan in a large roasting tin and add enough boiling water to come halfway up cake pan. Bake for about 30 minutes or until cake stays firm in center when gently shaken. Remove cake from water and cook 10 minutes. Unmold onto serving platter and cool completely. Dust with powdered sugar. Garnish with orange slices. Cake will be soft, almost pudding-like in texture.

1-1/2 cups sugar

1/2 cup water

2 tablespoons vanilla extract

8 oz. unsweetened chocolate, finely chopped

4 oz. semisweet chocolate, finely chopped

1 cup unsalted butter, softened

5 eggs, room temperature

Powdered sugar

Orange slices to garnish

Rose Water Cookies

🍂 Cream butter and sugar until light and fluffy. Add egg, beating well. Sift together flour, baking powder, baking soda and salt. Add to creamed mixture alternately with sour cream and rose water, beating until well blended. Divide dough in half, wrap each in plastic wrap and refrigerate for 4 hours or overnight. Preheat oven to 375F. On a well floured board (dough will be sticky), roll half of dough at a time 1/4-inch thick. Cut with a 2-1/2-inch heart-shaped cookie cutter. Sprinkle lightly with sugar. Place on a ungreased cookie sheet and bake for about 12 minutes or until light golden. Arrange on a doily-covered platter and decorate with rose buds.

1/2 cup unsalted butter, softened

3/4 cups sugar

1 egg

2-1/4 cups all-purpose flour

1/2 teaspoon baking powder

1/2 teaspoon baking soda

Pinch of salt

1/2 cup sour cream

1/2 tablespoon rose water

Sugar

Peppermint Creams

1 egg white

About 4 cups powdered
    sugar

A few drops peppermint
    extract

Mint leaves to garnish

🍃 Beat the egg white until frothy but not stiff.
Sift sugar and add enough to egg to form a stiff
mixture. Exactly how much you use depends
on the size of the egg. Add a few drops to taste
of peppermint. Knead to a firm paste and roll
out on a board lightly dusted with powdered
sugar. Cut into 1-inch rounds. Place in a single
layer on wax paper. Leave in a warm place for
24 hours to dry. Store excess in an airtight tin.
Arrange in a bonbon dish and garnish with
mint leaves.

Betrothal Shower

At modern bridal showers we give new gifts. The Victorians had a charming custom of bestowing "betrothal souvenirs." A female relative of the bride-to-be would hold a tea for her, and invite other women family members and intimate friends. The guests would bring some small but significant treasure: perhaps a single cup-and-saucer or platter left from grandmother's china, a piece of silver or linen, a faded photograph, an old brooch or locket, a postcard with a message from a long departed relative, a book, a purse, some preserved clothing. The gift would be accompanied by a written history and the name of every person to whom it belonged in the past. These records were entered into a souvenir book at the tea.

The Victorians believed that such a loving collection imparted a blessing, a charm, on the new home of the young bride. Often, she would keep this invaluable inheritance in a velvet-lined shelved cabinet to be displayed with pride.

The recipes for this betrothal tea for fifteen guests are low-calorie and low in fat. Much tea food is rich so it seemed prudent to include at least one light tea. The scones are so flavorful that you can eat them just as they are. But for those not concerned about weight-loss, they are equally delicious with butter or preserves.

Menu for Fifteen

Cucumber Dill Sandwiches

Mini Scones

Light-at-Hearts

Coffee Walnut Cake

Meringue Bonbons

Victoria's Treasure Lemon Tea

Cucumber Dill Sandwiches

2 English cucumbers
Salt to taste
8 tablespoons butter, softened
8 tablespoons diet mayonnaise
4 tablespoons fresh dill
32 slices thin cut white bread
Dill sprigs for garnishing

ᴈ• Cut the cucumbers into paper thin slices. Spread on paper towels. Sprinkle with salt and cover with more towels. Set aside for 15 minutes until moisture is absorbed. Combine butter, mayonnaise and dill and mix well. Remove crusts from bread and spread evenly and thinly with butter mixture. Place three layers of cucumber slices on 16 pieces of bread. Top with remaining bread slices. Cut each sandwich diagonally to make four triangles. Garnish with dill.

Mini Scones

2-1/2 cups all-purpose flour
2 teaspoons baking powder
1 teaspoon baking soda
1/2 teaspoon salt
1/2 cup sugar
6 tablespoons butter, chilled and cubed
1 egg, lightly beaten
About 1/2 cup low-fat buttermilk
Grated peel of 1/2 lemon
Milk for brushing on scones

ᴈ• Preheat oven to 425F. Lightly coat a large baking sheet with cooking spray. Sift first four ingredients together. Stir in sugar. With fingers, rub in butter until mixture is crumbly. With a fork, stir in egg, lemon peel and enough buttermilk to make a dough that barely holds together. Turn out onto a floured surface. Roll out with a floured rolling pin to make a round about 1/2 inch thick. Cut in rounds with a 1-inch cookie cutter. Place 1 to 1-1/2 inches apart on the baking sheet; brush lightly with milk. Bake 10 to 12 minutes or until scones are well risen and golden. Cool on a wire rack for 5 minutes. Serve immediately.

Light-at-Hearts

≈ Preheat oven to 325F. Line a 15 x 10 x 1-inch jellyroll tin with foil. Lightly coat with cooking spray. Dredge lightly with flour. Combine 3/4 cup flour, 1/4 cup plus 2 tablespoons sugar, cocoa, baking powder, baking soda, and salt. Make a well in center of mixture. Combine water, oil and liqueur; add to dry ingredients, stirring until blended. Set aside. Beat egg whites until foamy. Gradually add 1/4 cup plus 2 tablespoons sugar, beating until stiff peaks form. Fold 1/3 of egg mixture into chocolate. Fold in remaining egg mixture and remaining 1/4 cup flour. Pour into pan, spreading evenly. Bake for 25 minutes or until a wooden pick inserted in the center comes out clean. Cool 30 minutes on a wire rack. Invert tin and carefully peel foil away from cake. Cut into 15 hearts with a 2-1/2-inch heart-shaped cookie cutter. Dust with powdered sugar. Arrange on a doily covered platter and decorate with raspberries.

1 cup cake flour
3/4 cup sugar
1/3 cup unsweetened cocoa
1 teaspoon baking powder
1/2 teaspoon baking soda
Pinch salt
1/2 cup water
1/4 cup vegetable oil
2 teaspoons Grand Marnier
5 egg whites, room temperature
Powdered sugar and raspberries for garnishing

Coffee Walnut Cake

≈ Preheat oven to 375F. Lightly grease an 8-inch cake pan. Cream butter and sugar until light and fluffy. Add eggs 1 at a time, beating well. Stir in 1 tablespoon coffee. Combine flour, baking powder, and salt. Fold into creamed mixture. Stir in chopped walnuts. Pour into the pan and smooth top. Bake for 25 minutes or until top springs back when touched. Turn out on a wire rack. Cool completely. Combine powdered sugar and remaining teaspoon of coffee. Drizzle over cake and decorate with walnut halves.

1/2 cup butter, softened
1/2 cup sugar
2 eggs, beaten
1 tablespoon plus 1 teaspoon strong, black coffee
1 cup all-purpose flour
1-1/2 teaspoons baking powder
Pinch of salt
1/2 cup chopped walnuts
1 cup powdered sugar, sifted
12 walnut halves

Meringue Bonbons

2 egg whites, room
  temperature

2/3 cup sugar

1 teaspoon vanilla extract

Pinch of salt

1/2 cup semisweet
  chocolate pieces

1/2 chopped walnuts

❧ Preheat oven to 350F. Cover a large baking sheet with foil. Beat egg whites until foamy. Gradually add sugar and beat until stiff peaks form. Add vanilla and salt, then fold in chocolate and nuts. Drop by teaspoonfuls 2 inches apart on baking sheet. Put in oven then turn off heat and leave for at least 5 hours (overnight for convenience) without opening door. Cookies will be light brown. Store in an airtight tin until ready to serve.

Summer Picnic Tea

The Victorians had a great love of the outdoors. I can do no better than to reproduce these instructions from Mrs. Burton Kingsland on how to hold a great picnic tea.

"The ideal picnic should have the charm of things primitive and rustic; anything suggestive of artificial life should be banished. The best time to choose is late spring or early summer when the air is filled with refreshing coolness and delicate fragrance. Through interlacing boughs the sunshine is sifted in bright little patches on the white damask cloth. The bird orchestra furnishes the music, supplemented by merry human laughter.

"In choosing company for a picnic only those should be invited who can be counted upon for good nature, who are ready to laugh at trifling mishaps. One must be suitably clothed; no fashionable furbe-lows, but so dressed as to be utterly unconscious of one's attire.

"Most of the preparations for the feast must be made in advance, and all may be packed the night before, except the sandwiches, which should be freshly made. Sandwiches may be made with anything — cheese, sardines, paté-de-foie-gras, cold meats. Cakes require especially tender treatment — a sodden mass with crumbs adhering is the result of carelessness. Pies are not recommended. Fruit of all kinds, nuts and raisins, are sufficiently dainty.

"After the feast is over and the games and fun claim the attention of the party, there is generally a great lack of enthusiasm if it be suggested that there is any work to be done. But the eternal fitness of things require that one leaves the leafy paradise in the same orderly condition as when one invaded its solemn stillness."

Menu for Ten

Pressed Beef Sandwiches

Turnover Cookies

Almond Cherry Cake

Summer Fruit Salad

Victoria's Treasure Iced Passion Fruit Tea

Pressed Beef Sandwiches

3lb. brisket of beef

1/2 lb. salt pork

1 carrot, sliced

1 turnip, sliced

2 onions, each studded
with 4 cloves

12 peppercorns

Bunch of celery tops,
parsley and bay leaves

20 slices white bread

10 sweet pickles

&❧ Cover brisket with cold water. Bring slowly to the boil, then throw away water. Add remaining ingredients, cover with water and slowly bring to the boil. Reduce heat and simmer for 2-1/2 hours or until beef is tender. Remove beef and put between two plates with a heavy object on top. Leave in a cool place overnight. Next day, slice and place between two pieces of bread. Remove crusts and cut diagonally in two sandwiches. At picnic, serve with pickles.

Turnover Cookies

1-3/4 cups all-purpose
flour

1/2 cup potato flour

1/3 cup sugar

1/2 cup plus 5 tablespoons
butter, chilled and
cubed

1 egg

1/2 cup strawberry
preserves

1/3 cup coarsely crushed
sugar cubes

1/3 cup finely chopped
walnuts

1 egg white, lightly beaten

&❧ Sift flour and potato flour together. Add sugar. Cut in butter until mixture is crumbly. Add egg and mix to a soft dough. Gather into a ball and flatten into a circle. Wrap in plastic and refrigerate overnight. Divide dough in half and leave at room temperature for 15 minutes. Preheat oven to 350F. Line cookie sheets with parchment. Working with one half at a time, knead dough briefly to soften. Roll out between sheets of floured wax paper to thickness of 1/8 inch. Cut in circles with a 2-1/2-inch fluted cookie cutter. Place on baking sheet. Put 1/4 teaspoon preserves in center of each. Gently fold over half of cookie. Combine crushed sugar and nuts. Brush cookies with egg white and sprinkle with nut mixture. Bake for about 10 minutes or until pale golden. Cool on baking sheet for 10 minutes then transfer to wire rack to cool completely. Carry to picnic in a tin.

Almond Cherry Cake

🍂 Place cherries in a colander and pour over boiling water to wash off excess sugar and prevent cherries from sinking in the cake. Shake of excess water and dry cherries with paper towels. Allow to cool completely before using. Preheat oven to 275F. Grease an 8-inch cake pan and line with parchment paper. Cream butter, margarine and sugar until light and fluffy. Add eggs and almond extract and beat well. Stir in cherries. Combine flour, almonds, baking powder and salt, and fold into creamed mixture. Pour into pan and smooth top. Sprinkle with sugar. Bake for 1-1/2 to 2 hours or until a wooden pick inserted in center comes out clean. Cool in pan for 20 minutes, then turn out onto a wire rack. Cool completely before wrapping in foil to take to picnic.

1/2 cup candied cherries
1/2 cup butter
1/2 cup margarine
1 cup sugar
3 eggs, lightly beaten
1/4 teaspoon almond extract
2 cups all-purpose flour, sifted
1 cup ground almonds
1 teaspoon baking powder
1/4 teaspoon salt
1 tablespoon sugar

Summer Fruit Salad

🍂 Wash, stone and suitably prepare fruit. Combine in a bowl with a lid. Allow tea to go completely cold. Strain over fruit. Immediately before leaving for picnic, sprinkle on sugar and mix thoroughly. Snap on bowl lid to transport. Serve in picnic cups.

4 lbs. mixed red fruit: dark cherries, dark plums, raspberries, strawberries, as available
1 pt. Victoria's Treasure Earl Grey tea made 1-1/2 times stronger than usual
1 cup sugar

Iced Passion Fruit Tea

25 teaspoons Victoria's Treasure Passion Fruit Tea

20 cups cold water

Sugar

Ice

❧ Bring the water to a rolling boil. Make tea in the usual way, but slightly stronger than for hot tea. When it has brewed, strain into large, empty fruit juice or mason jars to transport to picnic. Sweeten to taste. Take ice cubes in a cooler. At picnic, fill plastic glasses 3/4 full with ice and pour on iced tea.

Alice in Wonderland Tea Party

How often have you seen little girls playing "tea party?" Young children love the concept, and the same was true in Victorian days. In 1869, Mary A. Cragin reminisced about a tea she remembered from her own childhood. "I read until the tea bell rang. As I went down stairs I saw the tea table set — a round table — and I thought round tables were so nice! We used a square one at home. There was a plate of smoking, hot biscuit, some strawberries and cream, a plate of seedcakes, a little round loaf of plum cake, and a custard pie. It was very tempting."

A tea is a wonderful idea for a children's birthday party, and an "Alice" tea is especially appropriate. Lewis Carroll, the author of "Alice in Wonderland" and "Alice Through the Looking Glass" was born in 1832 and died in 1898, so he lived almost his entire life within the reign of Victoria. His classic children's books feature tea and tea foods extensively. Remember the Mad Hatter's tea party and the stolen tarts? A quick look through the books will refresh your memory and give you lots of ideas for decorations.

Depending on the age of the children attending, you may or may not want to serve them tea. If you do, you might consider one of the decafinated options. In England, quite young children drink tea frequently. Usually it is served with milk. But if you wish, you can serve the tea in a separate room to sooth the frazzled parents, while the children stick to lemon barley water.

Menu for Six

Queen of Hearts Sandwiches

Fairy Cakes

The Stolen Tarts

"Eat Me" Cake

Lemon Barley Water

Victoria's Treasure Earl Grey Tea

Queen of Hearts Sandwiches

12 slices fresh white
    sandwich bread

3/4 cup Victoria's Treasure
    strawberry jam

ꝫ With a small heart-shaped candy cutter, or freehand with the tip of a sharp knife, cut heart-shaped holes in the middle of 6 bread slices. Spread jam evenly over remaining 6 slices. Place cut slices on top. Remove crusts, and trim sandwiches roughly to size of playing cards.

Fairy Cakes

1/4 cup all-purpose flour

1/2 cup cornstarch

1-1/2 teaspoons baking
    powder

1/4 cup butter

1/4 cup sugar

1 egg, beaten

1-2 tablespoons milk

1 cup powdered sugar

1 to 2 tablespoons warm
    water

Pink and green food
    coloring

ꝫ Preheat oven to 375F. Grease 12 shallow tartlet pans. Sift together first three ingredients. Cream butter and sugar until light and fluffy. Beat egg into the creamed mixture alternately with flour. Mix in enough milk to make a soft, dropping consistency. Spoon mixture evenly between pans. Bake for 7 to 10 minutes or until risen and springy to touch. Cool completely on a wire rack. Sift powdered sugar. Stir in water a little at a time to make a smooth, thick icing that coats the back of a metal spoon. Divide into two bowls. Put a drop of pink coloring in one, and green in the other. Mix well. Stand wire rack over paper towels to catch drips, and drizzle colored icing over fairy cakes.

The Stolen Tarts

1 recipe pastry (page 55)

1 recipe lemon curd
    (page 60)

1/2 cup powdered sugar.

ꝫ Preheat oven to 400F. Make tartlet shells as directed for fruit tarts. Bake for 5 minutes. Remove from oven and put 1-1/2 tablespoons lemon curd in each shell. Return to oven for a further 5 minutes, or until pastry is brown and lemon curd is bubby. Cool completely on a wire rack. Dust with powdered sugar.

"Eat Me" Cake

Preheat oven to 325F. Grease an 8-1/2 x 4-1/2 x 2-1/2-inch loaf pan. Cream butter, lemon peel and sugar until light and fluffy. Beat in lemon juice and vanilla. Add eggs one at a time, beating well. Sift together flour, baking powder and salt. Add to cream mixture alternately with milk, beating well. Stir in coconut. Bake for 1 hour and 20 minutes, or until a wooden pick insterted in center comes out clean. Cool in pan for 20 minutes. Remove and cool completely on a wire rack. Spear currents on a toothpick and dip into jam. Using jam as adhesive, spell out the words "EAT ME" in currents on top of the cake.

1/2 cup butter, softened
1/2 teaspoon grated lemon peel
3/4 cup sugar
2 tablespoons lemon juice
1 teaspoon vanilla
3 eggs
1-1/2 cups all-purpose flour
1/2 teaspoon baking powder
3/4 teaspoon salt
1/2 cup milk
1/2 cup flaked coconut
Currents
Jam

Lemon Barley Water

Place barley in a sieve and pour boiling water over to clean it. Place clean barley, cold water and lemon rind in a pan with a lid. Simmer for 30 minutes. Strain into a pitcher and add lemon juice and sugar to taste. Serve within 24 hours.

6 oz. pearl barley
4 pts. cold water
3 strips of lemon rind
Juice of 1-1/2 lemons
3 tablespoons sugar

Graduation Tea

Victorian debutantes could expect to have a coming out cotillion, a swell event that lasted well into the night and ended with a late supper. On a less grand and more intimate note, she could also expect her mother to hold a tea just for women friends to introduce the daughter to the adult social world. The young woman — known as a "bud" during her first year in society — would "receive" with her mother for the first time at this tea.

Such as tea was thus described: "The informal service of this afternoon tea is its charm, a friend presiding at the urn, and young girls with their sweet faces and pretty dresses assisting. Whether of the rose family or those of society, buds are very attractive, very fair to see."

Except in the highest echelons of society, young women today no longer "come out." But someone you know might love to have an elegant tea when she graduates from high school or college, which is after all, often the sign of reaching adulthood in today's world.

Invite the young woman's female classmates, family and friends. In keeping with the "bud" theme, decorate the room with rose buds. Make a small presentation of a small graduation gift — perhaps a crystal bud vase — which can be kept as a keepsake of this special occasion.

As a side note, the sponge cake featured in this menu was named for Queen Victoria. When her consort, Prince Albert died in 1861, Victoria became something of a recluse. She was coaxed back into society by way of a series of tea-parties at which this cake was served.

Menu for Twenty

Ribbon-Tied Sandwhiches

Currant Scones with Blackberry Butter

Victoria Sponge Cake

Nut Fudge

Blackberry Sherbert

Victoria's Treasure Darjeeling Tea

Ribbon-Tied Sandwiches

2 bunches green onions

1 cup cooked bay shrimp

1/2 cup butter, softened

1/8 teaspoon cayenne pepper

Salt to taste

About 1/4 cup tarragon vinegar

20 slices fresh, white sandwich bread sliced thin

ʑ•Cut the white end from onions and reserve for another purpose. Wash and trim green leaves. Boil a pan of water and drop onion greens in for one minute. Lift out of water and drain on paper towels. Set aside on fresh towel until completely cool and dry. Puree shrimp in a food processor or blender. Thoroughly mix to a paste with butter. Add seasonings and vinegar to taste. Trim crusts from bread. Spread shrimp mixture on each slice of bread. Carefully roll each slice starting from a long side. Refrigerate for 30 minutes. Tie each sandwich in the center with an onion leaf. Arrange on a platter and decorate with flowers.

Currant Scones

2-2/3 cups unbleached all-purpose flour

6 tablespoons sugar

1-1/2 teaspoons baking powder

1/2 teaspoon baking soda

1/4 teaspoon salt

3/4 cup unsalted butter, chilled and cubed

1-1/2 cups currants

1/2 cup buttermilk

6 tablespoons whipping cream

1 egg, lightly beaten

ʑ•Preheat oven to 325F. Lightly grease a baking sheet. Combine first 5 ingredients. Cut in butter until mixture is crumbly. Add currants. Combine buttermilk and cream. Make a well in center of dry mixture and add liquid. Stir with a knife until dough gathers together. With floured hands, form dough into a smooth ball. Roll out on a floured board to 3/4-inch thick. Cut out with a 2-inch cookie cutter. Place on baking sheet. Brush tops with beaten egg. Bake for 25 minutes or until golden brown. Cool on a wire rack. Serve immediately with blackberry butter.

Blackberry Butter

6 tablespoons unsalted butter, softened

1/3 cup Victoria's Treasure blackberry jelly

ʑ•Blend butter and jelly until smooth. Pack into decorative dish and refrigerate. Soften slightly before serving.

Victoria Sponge Cake

Preheat oven to 350F. Grease 4 round 8-inch cake pans. Sift flour, stir in lemon peel. Cream butter and sugar until light and fluffy. Beat in eggs 1 at a time. Fold in flour. Divide between pans, spreading evenly. Bake 25 minutes or until top of cake springs back when lightly touched. Cool in pans a few minutes, then turn out onto a wire rack to cool completely. Sandwich two layers together with jam to make two cakes. Place 8-inch paper doilies on top of the cakes and lightly sift powdered sugar over them. Carefully remove the doily, leaving a lacy pattern on the cakes. Cut in wedges to serve.

3 cups all-purpose flour
4 teaspoons baking powder
Grated peel of 2 lemon
1-1/2 cups butter, softened
1-1/2 cups sugar
6 eggs
2/3 cup raspberry jam
Powdered sugar

Nut Fudge

Grease an 8-inch square baking pan. Heat sugar, water and margarine over low heat until sugar dissolves. Increase heat and bring to a boil. Add milk and boil 30 to 40 minutes or until mixture is thick. (One drop cooled on a greased pan should feel thick and tacky when pinched.) Meanwhile, grind nuts until mixture resembles cornmeal. Remove milk mixture from heat and stir in coloring. Add nuts and stir for about 3 minutes or until mixture stiffens slightly. Pour into pan and smooth top. Score into squares with a greased knife. Cool completely. Cut into squares. Place in paper candy cases and arrange in bonbon dishes. Decorate with mint leave and a few whole nuts.

3/4 cup sugar
3/4 cup water
1 teaspoon margarine
3/4 cup milk
1/2 cup unsalted cashews
1/2 cup raw almonds
1/2 cup shelled, unsalted pistachios
4 drops green food coloring
Mint leaves and nuts to garnish

Blackberry Tea Sherbert

2 cups cold Victoria's
 Treasure blackberry tea
1 cup sugar
8 cups fresh blackberries
3 teaspoons lemon juice
1-1/2 cups milk
Blackberries to garnish

❧ Heat tea and sugar over a low flame until sugar dissolves. Turn up heat and bring to boil. Remove from heat and cool. Wash berries and puree. Strain to remove seeds. Combine with tea mixture and lemon juice. Stir in milk. Pour into 2 8-inch square pans. Freeze 4 hours or until firm, stirring occasionally. Serve small scoops in pretty dessert cups.

Wedding Garden Party

The tradition of garden tea parties dates back to the sixteenth century, and continues today in the form of the Queen's garden parties at Buckingham Palace.

A garden tea is a delightful way to celebrate a summer wedding. The refreshments can be served buffet style from a large table tastefully arranged with flowers, a single color predominating.

The bridal cake is a must according to "What to Serve and How to Prepare It," a late Victorian-era cookbook. "This time-honored dainty is an indispensable feature of the properly conducted wedding; but it is now , as formerly cut and eaten in the course of the wedding feast, the modern fashion being to have the cake cut into small wedges and packed in dainty white boxes, tied up with white ribbon, previous to the ceremony. The old custom of placing a gold ring and a silver thimble in the cake is still occasionally observed, but when this is done the cake is cut and distributed by the bride herself at the close of the wedding. The guest to whom the ring falls is supposed to be destined to speedy marriage, while she who secures the silver thimble is positively ordained to spinsterhood."

Menu for Thirty

Open-Faced Smoked Salmon Sandwiches

Pecan Shortbread

Raspberry Tarts

Maids of Honor

Chocolate Truffles

Victorian Wedding Cake

Victoria's Treasure Earl Grey Tea

Champagne

Open-Faced
Smoked Salmon Sandwiches

2 1-lb loaves of firm dark
  bread
1/4 lb thin sliced smoked
  salmon
1/2 cup creme fraich
2 tablespoons finely
  chopped fresh dill
Lemon slices to garnish

≈ Cut bread into circles with a 1-1/2-inch fluted cookie cutter. Top each with a slice of smoked salmon, a dab of creme fraich and sprinkle with dill. Garnish with lemon slices.

Pecan Shortbread

2 cups all-purpose flour
1/2 cup firm packed
  brown sugar
5-1/2 tablespoons corn-
  starch
1 teaspoon cinnamon
1/4 teaspoon salt
1 cup unsalted butter,
  chilled and cubed
1 teaspoon vanilla extract
1 cup pecans, finely
  chopped

≈ Preheat oven to 375F. Mix first five ingredients. Add butter and vanilla and cut in until mixture is crumbly. Add pecans. Turn out onto a sheet of wax paper. Knead until dough adheres. Divide into two balls. Set one aside. Top other with another sheet of wax paper and roll into a 10-inch round. Peel off top sheet. Invert into an 11-inch tart pan and press dough to fit. Cut, all the way through, into 16 wedges. Prick with fork. Repeat with other half. Bake about 20 minutes or until shortbread is golden brown. Recut wedges. Cool in pan on wire rack. Arrange on platters and decorate with flowers.

Raspberry Tarts

❧ Sift flour and salt. Stir in sugar. Cut in butter until mixture is crumbly. Mix egg yolks and lemon juice. Add to flour and mix with a knife until dough comes away cleanly from sides of bowl. If necessary, add water a little at a time to obtain correct consistency. Turn out onto a lightly floured surface and knead very lightly just until dough holds together. Wrap and refrigerate 30 minutes. Preheat oven to 400F. Grease 30 2-inch tartlet pans. On a lightly floured surface, roll out pastry thinly. Cut into 30 rounds with a 3-inch cookie cutter. Line pans with pastry. Prick bottoms lightly with a fork. Bake about 10 minutes or until golden brown. Carefully remove from pans and cool completely on a wire rack. Dust rims of shells with powdered sugar. Arrange raspberries attractively in shells. In a small saucepan, stir jelly over low heat just until melted. Using a pastry brush, glaze fruit completely. Cool before serving. Garnish with mint sprigs.

4 cups all-purpose flour
1/4 teaspoon salt
2 tablespoons sugar
1 cup butter, chilled and cubed
2 egg yolks
4 teaspoons lemon juice
About 2 tablespoons cold water, if needed
1/2 cup powdered sugar
1-1/2 cups fresh raspberries
3/4 cup red current jelly
Mint sprigs to garnish

Maids of Honor

❧ Preheat oven to 350F. Grease 30 2-inch tartlet pans. Make pastry shells as directed above, but do not bake. Cream butter and sugar until light and fluffy. Beat in eggs. Stir in brandy. Gently but thoroughly fold in flour. Spoon mixture into tartlet shells. Bake 20 to 25 minutes or until pastry is browned and filling springs back when lightly touched. Cool completely on wire racks. Dust with powdered sugar before serving.

1 recipe pastry, see above
1/2 cup butter, softened
1/2 cup sugar
2 eggs
2 teaspoons brandy
1 cup all-purpose flour
3 tablespoons powdered sugar

Chocolate Truffles

8 oz. semisweet chocolate

6 tablespoons unsalted butter

1/2 cup powdered sugar, sifted

1/4 cup unsweetened cocoa

Break the chocolate into the top of a double boiler over hot water. Slowly melt chocolate. When melted, remove from water. Add butter and stir to melt. Stir in powdered sugar. Set aside for 20 minutes to firm. Form into 30 balls and roll in cocoa powder. Place in paper cases and arrange in pretty candy dishes.

Victorian Wedding Cake

1 pound butter

2 cups light-brown sugar

9 eggs, separated

1 cup cold Victoria's Treasure Assam tea

4 cups all-purpose flour

1/2 teaspoon baking soda

1 teaspoon mace

1/2 teaspoon nutmeg

2 teaspoons cinnamon

3 lbs. currents

2 lbs. seedless raisins

1 lb. citron

1/2 lb. almonds, chopped

Preheat oven to 275F. Grease 2 deep 9-inch cake pans and line with wax paper. Cream the butter until light and fluffy. Add the sugar gradually while beating. Beat egg yolks until thick and light. Add to butter mixture. Whisk whites until stiff. Fold into mixture. Add tea. Sift flour with spices and soda and gradually beat into mixture. Stir in fruit and nuts. Pour into cake pans and bake for about 3-1/2 hours, or until a wooden pick inserted in the center comes out clean. Cool in pans on wire racks. When cool, turn out and peel off paper. Cut in wedges and package in small, ribbon-tied boxes.

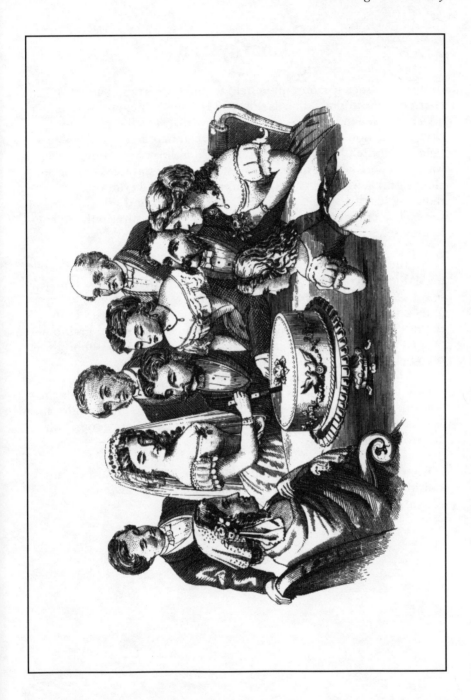

Charity Tea

Victorian society ladies often held theme tea parties in aid of charitable institutions such as the local Home for Incurables. Holding a Victorian tea today is an excellent way to raise revenues for your club, association or favorite cause. Described here is a "Rainbow" tea held at a church hall in Philadelphia. "From the center of the room, where they are caught in graceful festoons, hang soft folds of colored cloth — pink, white, blue, yellow, brown, green and crimson — radiating like the spokes of a wheel to the corners and sides of the room. The other ends of the bunting hang over booths similar in color to themselves.

"At the white booth are the angel cakes. Not more snowy white are the daisies which decorate this booth than these delicate cakes themselves, resting on banks of fern, and sold by two girls in white." The other colored booths are described in similar fashion. Then, "in the center of the room, under an immense Japanese umbrella, a rainbow-dressed maiden dispenses tea, and at the other side of the umbrella, to keep her company, is another damsel selling lemonade."

Given here are recipes for the yellow booth, but with some imagination you will come up with appropriate dishes for the other colors: for instance, berry tarts on the crimson table, and chocolate goodies on the brown one.

Each guest pays for a cup, which can be refilled with tea, and buys individual portions of cake or other dainties. Whole cakes and recipes also can be sold.

Menu for One Booth

Open-Faced Egg Sandwiches

Scones with Lemon Curd

Orange Cake

Butter Cookies

Peanut Butter Bonbons

Open-Faced Egg Sandwiches

5 hard-boiled eggs
5 tablespoons mayonnaise
2-1/2 tablespoons Dijon mustard
Salt and pepper to taste
1 small bunch watercress
1 1-lb. sliced loaf of day-old white bread

🍂 Roughly chop eggs. Add mayonnaise, mustard and seasoning. Mash to a smooth paste with a fork. Wash, drain and pat dry watercress. Coarsely chop half, and stir in egg mixture. Cut crusts off bread slices. Cut bread in circles using a 2-inch cookie cutter. Pile egg mixture on bread. Garnish with remaining watercress sprigs.

Scones with Lemon Curd

Grated peel of 4 lemons
Juice of 4 lemons (about 1 cup)
1/2 cup butter, cubed
2 cups sugar
1 recipe scones (page 32)

🍂 In the top of a large double boiler, combine lemon peel, lemon juice, eggs, butter and sugar. Place over simmering water and stir until sugar is dissolved. Continue to cook, stirring occasionally, until thickened and smooth. While hot, pour into hot sterilized 1/2 pint canning jars, leaving about 1/8-inch headspace. Run a narrow spatula down between lemon curd and side of jar to release air. Top with sterilized lids; firmly screw on bands. Place in draft-free area to cool. Make the scones as directed. Split, and serve spread with lemon curd.

Orange Cake

ᵊ Preheat oven to 350F. Generously grease a 10-cut Bundt pan. Cream butter and sugar until light and fluffy. Beat in eggs one at a time, beating well. Add vanilla, orange juice and orange rind. Blend yogurt and baking soda in small bowl; add to creamed mixture alternately with flour. Pour into pan. Bake 45 to 50 minutes or until a wooden pick inserted in cake comes out clean. Cool in pan on wire rack about 40 minutes. Turn out on rack and cool completely. Combine all remaining ingredients and beat until smooth. Drizzle over cake. Serve by the slice.

1 cup butter, softened
3 cups granulated sugar
5 eggs
1 teaspoon vanilla
1/4 cup orange juice
1-1/2 tablespoons grated orange rind
1 8-oz. container plain yogurt
1/2 teaspoon baking soda
2-3/4 cups all-purpose flour
1 tablespoon butter, softened
1 egg yolk
2 cups powdered sugar
1 teaspoon grated orange rind
1/2 cup orange juice

Butter Cookies

ᵊ Preheat oven to 375F. Lightly grease a baking sheet. Sift together flour, baking powder and salt. Cut in butter until mixture is crumbly. Stir in sugar and raisins. Beat egg and milk together. Stir into mixture to form a soft dough. Roll out on a floured board to 1/4-inch thick. Cut out with a 2-inch round cookie cutter. Place on baking sheet well spaced. Bake for 15 minutes or until light golden brown. Cool on baking sheet for 2 minutes then transfer to a wire rack to cool completely.

2 cups all-purpose flour
2 teaspoons baking powder
1/4 teaspoon salt
1/2 cup butter
1/2 cup sugar
2/3 cup seedless golden raisins
1 egg
2 tablespoons milk

Peanut Butter Bonbons

2 cups chunky peanut
butter

1/2 cup butter

4-1/2 cups powdered
sugar, sifted

3 cups crisp rice cereal,
crushed

1 12-oz. package butter-
scotch pieces

Place peanut butter and butter together over a low heat until melted. Stir to blend. Combine sugar and cereal. Pour butter mixture over dry mixture. Blend together with hands. Form into 1-inch diameter balls. Chill until firm. Cover a baking sheet with wax paper. Melt butterscotch pieces in top of a double boiler over hot water. Dip bonbons into butterscotch and swirl as you withdraw them. Place on baking sheet and chill until firm. Place in paper candy cases to sell.

Family Sunday Tea

In many Victorian homes, children were raised on a day-to-day basis by a nanny (remember Mary Poppins?). Young children took their evening meal in front of the nursery fire before going to bed. Often, this was the one hour of the day parents spent with their children.

Sunday was special because the servants were off. According to a Mrs. M.C. Myer writing in 1894, Sunday evening tea was "one of the most delightful meals of the week, frequently prepared by the mistress herself and therefore distinguished for its dainty prettiness, both in menu and service. A favorite family dish is a pleasure, and somehow has a different flavor when prepared by the hands of love. How free and unrestrained the conversation on this day of all others. Grown children (from homes of their own) come 'home' to receive the loving welcome always awaiting them. While Sunday tea remains a household feature, home love will flourish and its dear ones never go very far astray."

We're in another era now when both parents often work and family get-togethers are difficult to arrange. Perhaps a family Sunday tea can become a tradition in your home. This menu is in the tradition of high tea, a more complete meal than afternoon tea.

Kids love tea foods. Let them help with making cookies or toasting the crumpets. While the adults drink their Darjeeling, serve the little ones hot chocolate.

Menu for Six

Eggs in Overcoats

Toasted Crumpets

Baked Apple Pudding

Almond Sugar Cookies

Victoria's Treasure Darjeeling Tea

Hot Chocolate

Eggs in Overcoats

6 medium potatoes

1/4 cup milk, warmed

3 tablespoons chopped ham

2 tablespoons chopped parsley

2 tablespoons butter, softened

2 tablespoons heavy cream

Salt and pepper to taste

6 eggs plus 2 whites

1 tablespoon white vinegar

2 tablespoons grated Cheddar cheese

ᘏ Preheat oven to 400F. Scrub and prick potatoes. Bake them for about 55 minutes, depending on size. Cool for 15 minutes. Lay potatoes flat and slice top off each. Carefully scoop out potato flesh into a bowl and reserve skins. Mash potato with warm milk until smooth. Add ham, parsley, butter, cream and seasonings. Beat the egg white until stiff, and fold into potato mixture. Keep warm. Poach eggs in water and vinegar. When cooked, drain carefully. Half fill potato skins with potato mixture. Place a poached egg on each. Cover with remaining potato. Sprinkle with grated cheese. Brown quickly under a hot broiler.

Toasted Crumpets

1-1/2 cup all-purpose flour

1/2 (1/4-oz.) package active dry yeast

3/4 cup warm (110F) water

1/4 teaspoon baking soda

1/2 teaspoon salt

1/2 cup milk

Butter and Victoria's Treasure honey

ᘏ Combine flour and yeast. Add water and mix well. Cover with plastic wrap and let stand in a warm place for 1 hour or until batter has doubled in bulk and is puffy. Dissolve baking soda and salt in milk and add to batter. Stir vigorously until well mixed and batter is runny. Preheat a griddle or heavy skillet. Grease lightly. Also grease poached egg or English muffin rings. If you don't have any, improvise by cutting the tops and bottoms off well-washed 6-1/2-ounce tuna cans. Warm the rings on the griddle. Pour about 2 tablespoons batter into each ring. Reduce heat to low and cook about 7 minutes or until underside is browned and top covered with bubbles. Carefully remove rings. Turn and cook crumpets 2 to 3 minutes or until lightly browned. Regrease skillet and rings and repeat until batter is finished. Makes about 12 crumpets. Cool completely on wire rack. Reheat by toasting both sides under broiler, or over fire on a toasting fork. Serve warm with butter and honey.

Baked Apple Pudding

Preheat oven to 375F. Grease six 6-ounce ramekins. Beat butter and sugar until creamy. Beat in egg, then flour and baking powder until well mixed. Add milk and continue mixing until batter is smooth and light. Peel and core apples and cut into 1/4-inch pieces. Fold apple and spices into batter. Fill ramekins half full and place on a baking sheet. Bake 30 minutes or until tops are golden brown and a wooden pick inserted in the center comes out clean. Cool for 20 minutes. Unmold and serve warm.

6 tablespoons unsalted butter, softened

1/4 cup sugar

1 egg, room temperature

1/2 cup all-purpose flour

1/2 teaspoon baking powder

1/4 cup milk, room temperature

1 large Granny Smith Apple

1/2 teaspoon cinnamon

1/2 teaspoon ground ginger

Almond Sugar Cookies

Cream butter until light and fluffy. Add powdered sugar and beat until light. Mix in egg, almond extract and milk. Sift in flour, baking powder and salt. Mix until just blended. Gather dough into ball; flatten into a circle. Wrap and chill until firm, about 1 hour. Preheat oven to 350F. Grease baking sheets. Roll dough out between sheets of waxed paper to thickness of 1/16 inch. Remove top sheet of paper. Cut into 2-1/2-inch rounds, or in shapes of your choice. Sprinkle with sugar. Bake about 15 minutes or until golden brown. Cool completely on wire racks.

1/2 cup unsalted butter, softened

1 cup powdered sugar

1 egg

1 teaspoon almond extract

3/4 tablespoon milk

2 cups sifted flour

2 teaspoons baking powder

Pinch of salt

Sugar for sprinkling

Hot Chocolate

1/4 cup cocoa
1/8 cup flour
1/4 cup sugar
Pinch of salt
2 cups water
2 cups milk
1/4 teaspoon vanilla
  extract
Whipped cream, if desired

❧ Combine dry ingredients. Make a smooth paste with a few tablespoons of the water. Pour on remaining water. In a saucepan over medium heat bring to the boil and simmer for 15 minutes. Add milk. Return to a boil then remove from heat. Stir in vanilla. Pour into mugs and top with whipped cream, if desired.

Candlelight Gypsy Tea

The Victorians were fascinated with psychic phenomena and fortune telling. They often held sceances and consulted palm or crystal ball readers. In that vein this entertainment is a little out of the usual order of the social function termed a tea. The idea is to find someone among your acquaintances who is adept at reading tea leaves; or, since this fortune-telling tea is all in fun, find a book on the subject and use it as a guide to read for each other.

Tea leaf reading is an old form of soothsaying that apparently originated in Ireland. According to Irish tradition, no money should be asked for a tea cup reading. The saying is "'Tis a matter of hospitality and friendship. For to drink tea with one is to make him your friend."

Here's how it works. Pour tea from the pot into your cup without straining. Drink the tea from your cup, leaving but a teaspoonful of the beverage remaining on the leaves. Holding the cup upright in your right hand, swirl the cup three times counter-clockwise then turn it upside down on the saucer to train for a minute. The reader then interprets the pattern of leaves distributed around the cup.

Hold your Gypsy tea by candlelight, it is softer and more becoming, and adds to the atmosphere of the occasion.

Menu for Six

Welsh Rarebit

Coconut Cupcakes

Seedy Cake

Ginger Snaps

Victoria's Treasure Assam Tea

Sherry (optional)

Welsh Rarebit

6 slices of whole wheat
  bread
3 tablespoons butter
1-1/2 teaspoons English
  mustard
Fresh ground black pepper
12 oz. Stilton or Cheddar
  cheese
3 teaspoons red wine

❧ Toast the bread on both sides and butter one side. Spread with mustard and season with pepper. Arrange the slices in a single layer, butter side up, in an ovenproof dish or broiler pan. Slice the cheese and arrange on the toast. Sprinkle with red wine. Broil until cheese is bubbly. Serve immediately.

Coconut Cupcakes

1/3 cup dry curd cottage
  cheese
1 tablespoon light corn
  syrup
1 teaspoon milk
2 tablespoon flaked
  coconut
3/4 teaspoon coconut
  flavoring, divided
1/4 cup butter, softened
1/2 cup sugar
1 egg
1-1/4 cups all-purpose
  flour
3 tablespoons cocoa
  powder
1/2 teaspoon baking soda
Pinch of salt
2/3 cup milk

❧ Preheat oven to 375F. Put paper cupcake liners in 12 muffin pans. Beat first three ingredients together until smooth. Stir in coconut and half of coconut flavoring. Set aside. Cream butter and sugar until light and fluffy. Add egg and beat well. Sift together flour, cocoa, baking soda and salt. Add to cream mixture alternately with milk. Beat well. Stir in remaining coocnut flavoring. Spoon 2 tablespoons batter into each muffin cup; spoon 2 teaspoons coconut mixture on top. Divide remaining batter evenly between cakes over coconut mixture. Bake for 20 minutes. Remove from pan and cool on a wire rack.

Seedy Cake

❧ Preheat oven to 325F. Grease and line with parchment paper an 8-inch cake pan. Cream together butter and all but 3 teaspoons sugar until light and fluffy. Alternately beat in eggs and flour, ending with flour. Stir in all but 1/2 teaspoon caraway seeds. Pour into pan. Smooth top and sprinkle with remaining sugar and caraway seeds. Bake for 1-3/4 hours or until a wooden pick inserted in center comes out clean. Cool in pan for 10 minutes. Turn out onto a wire rack and cool completely. Serve on a pedestal cake stand.

1 cup butter
1 cup sugar
4 eggs, beaten
2 cups all-purpose flour
2 teaspoons baking powder
4 teaspoons caraway seeds

Ginger Snaps

❧ Grease a baking sheet. Sift the flour and combine with sugar, salt, baking soda and ginger. Heat the margarine, butter and syrup until melted. Cool slightly then stir into dry ingredients. Stir in egg, shape into a ball, wrap in plastic and chill for 1 hour. Break off walnut size pieces of dough and roll on a lightly floured board. Place on baking sheet and bake for 10 minutes or until firm. Cool completely on a wire rack.

2 cups all-purpose flour
1 cup soft dark brown sugar
1/2 teaspoon baking soda
1 teaspoon ground ginger
3 tablespoons margarine
2 tablespoons butter
1/3 cup light corn syrup
1 egg, lightly beaten

Christmas Eve Tea

"It was always said of him, that he knew how to keep Christmas well."

Charles Dickens 1812-1870

When we think of a traditional Christmas we often conjure up pictures of the sugar plums, caroling, and snowy sleigh rides that were typical of a Victorian holiday. Many of our most treasured Christmas customs originated in the mid-1800s. When the young queen married Prince Albert in 1840, he introduced the German custom of decking a fir tree with ribbons and candles and candies. Before a tree stood twinkling in the window, Christmas decorations had consisted of holly and ivy garlands collected from the woods. Victorians also began the practice of exchanging Christmas cards around 1846.

At a Christmas Eve tea, both children and adults played games such as blind man's buff or dumb crambo — a type of charades — and indulged in theatricals and strenuous dancing. Tea would include some traditional favorites such as mince tarts,

After the tea and festivities they might have a glass of wassail. The winter ritual of wassailing the trees — blessing them to encourage them bear more fruit — predates Christianity. By Victorian times, hot wassail punch was served around a blazing fire, and also handed out as a cheering cup to chilly carolers.

Menu for Ten

Ham Filled Savory Scones

Fruited Tea Cake

Glazed Gingerbread Men

Holiday Sherry Trifle

Wassail

Victoria's Treasure Cinnamon Tea

Ham Filled Savory Scones

1 cup all-purpose flour

1-1/2 teaspoons baking powder

1 teaspoon dry mustard

Pinch of salt

1 cup whole wheat flour

3 tablespoons butter, chilled and cubed

3/4 cup grated sharp Cheddar cheese

About 2/3 cup milk

Butter

Smoked ham

Chutney

Preheat oven to 425F. Lightly grease a baking sheet. Sift all-purpose flour, baking powder, mustard and salt. Stir in whole wheat flour. Cut in butter until mixture is crumbly. Stir in half a cup of cheese. Make a well in center of mixture and add enough milk to make a dough that barely holds together. Knead lightly on a floured board. Roll out to 3/4-inch thick circle. Cut into rounds with a 2-inch cookie cutter. Place on baking sheet. Sprinkle with remaining cheese. Bake 8 to 10 minutes or until well risen and golden. Cool on a wire rack. When room temperature, split and butter each half. Place a piece of ham and a 1/4 teaspoonful of chutney on each half. Arrange on a serving platter and decorate with Christmas foliage.

Fruited Tea Cake

1 cup cold Victoria's Treasure Darjeeling tea

1/2 cup butter

1/2 cup golden seedless raisins

1/2 cup currents

1 cup chopped dates

1 cup lightly packed brown sugar

2 cups all-purpose flour

2 rounded teaspoons baking powder

1 teaspoon baking soda

1/2 teaspoon ground cinnamon

1/4 teaspoon ground ginger

1/4 teaspoon ground nutmeg

Preheat oven to 350F. Grease and line with parchment paper a 9-inch cake pan. Combine tea, butter, fruit and sugar and heat over a low flame. Bring to the boil, stirring occasionally. Simmer for 3 minutes then remove from heat and allow to completely cool. Stir dry ingredients into fruit mixture. Thoroughly combine. Pour into cake pan and bake for about 1 hour or until a wooden pick inserted in center comes out clean. Cake can be made a couple of days in advance and stored in an airtight tin. Serve on a pedestal cake stand.

Glazed Gingerbread Men

≈ Sift flour, baking soda, salt, ginger, cinnamon and cloves together. Bring molasses to a boil and add sugar, margarine and milk. Stir until margarine is melted. Make a well in center of dry ingredients. Pour in molasses mixture and stir to make a soft dough. Cover and refrigerate for 1 hour. Preheat oven to 375F. Grease a baking sheet. Roll out dough to a thickness of 1/8-inch on a floured board. Cut out cookies with a gingerbread man cookie cutter. Place on baking sheet and bake for 8 to 10 minutes or until brown. Cool on a wire rack. Sift the powdered sugar and mix with lemon juice. Add a little water if necessary to make a spreading consistency. Spread over cookies. Make eyes with raisins. Set out on a tray lined with a doily.

2 cups all-purpose flour
1/2 teaspoon baking soda
1/2 teaspoon salt
1/2 teaspoon ground ginger
1/2 teaspoon ground cinnamon
1/2 teaspoon ground cloves
1/2 cup molasses
1/4 cup sugar
3 tablespoons margarine
1 tablespoon milk
2 cups powdered sugar
2 tablespoons lemon juice
Raisins

Holiday Sherry Trifle

1 recipe Victoria Sponge
(page 49)

2 cups whole milk

4 eggs

2 tablespoons sugar

1/2 teaspoon vanilla
extract

1/2 cup Victoria's Treasure
strawberry jam

1/2 cup cream sherry

2 cups whipping cream

Halved, blanched almonds

Gold dragees

ೆ Make cake according to directions and set aside to cool. Heat milk in a heavy saucepan over low heat until very hot but not boiling. Meanwhile, beat eggs, sugar and vanilla together. Pour hot milk in a thin stream over eggs, stirring constantly. Mix well then pour back into saucepan. Stir over medium heat until custard thickens enough to coat the back of a metal spoon. Pour into a clean bowl, cover and refrigerate until cool. Cut cake into pieces about 1 x 3-inches. Spread tops and bottoms with jam. Arrange in the bottom of a deep, decorative bowl. Slowly pour sherry over cake; tip bowl so cake absorbs all sherry. Pour cold custard sauce over cake and smooth top. Beat cream until it holds stiff peaks. Spread 3/4 of cream over custard. Put remainder in a pastry bag fitted with a star nozzle. Pipe cream in rosettes around edge of trifle. Decorate with almonds and dragees.

Wassail

4 very small red apples

1/2 cup soft brown sugar

2 pts. dark beer

1/2 pt. dry sherry

1/4 teaspoon ground
cinnamon

1/4 teaspoon grated
nutmeg

1/4 teaspoon ground
ginger

Strip of lemon peel

ೆ Preheat oven to 350F. Slit skin around center of apples and put them in a large flameproof bowl. Add sugar and 4 tablespoons of beer. Cover and bake for 20 to 30 minutes or until apples are tender. Remove apples from bowl and reserve. Add ale and sherry to bowl. Stir in spices and lemon peel. Bring to a boil on top of stove then turn down heat and simmer gently for 5 minutes. Pour into a heatproof punch bowl. Float apples in wassail, and serve immediately.

Farmhouse High Tea

There is often confusion between afternoon tea — a strictly social occasion with mainly sweet offerings — and high tea. Despite its patrician sounding name, high tea was actually a working class meal eaten in the early evening when the men came home from the fields and before the young children went to bed.

During the industrial revolution, when people moved to urban areas to work in factories and mills, they continued the tradition of having "tea" around five o'clock and a light supper just before bedtime.

Weekday high teas were generally kept to the immediate family, and were a "sit-down" meal usually taken around the kitchen table in front of a blazing hearth upon which the tea kettle was heated and the bread or scones toasted. On weekends or holidays high tea became a social affair with friends or extended family coming by.

During the week, high tea usually consisted of fairly simple fare such as leftover cold meats, muffins or crumpets, a simple cake, and perhaps a dessert such as fruit and gelatin. In the most poor homes, tea often meant nothing more than thick slices of bread with jam or honey. For company, a more elaborate "slap up" tea was served, perhaps Cornish pasties, scotch eggs, or sausage rolls served with relishes and chutney as well as salads. Always there was an endless supply of a good strong brew of tea.

A hearty farmhouse high tea is an ideal way to entertain when you have guests of all ages to consider. It is perfect for children as well as the elderly. Think of hosting a high tea for a wedding anniversary, a family reunion or on a holiday.

Menu for Six

English Farmhouse Salad

Hearty Bacon Scones

Yorkshire Apple Tart

Date Bars

Suspended Grapes

Victoria's Treasure Assam Tea

English Farmhouse Salad

1 large head crisp lettuce, shredded

1 small English cucumber, peeled and sliced

6 celery stalks, diced

6 scallions, chopped

6 tomatoes, quartered

6 hard-boiled eggs, quartered

1 large carrot, grated

4 tablespoons watercress, chopped

creamy salad dressing of your choice

ε•Combine first five ingredients in a salad bowl. Place tomatoes and eggs on top. Arrange grated carrot in a ring around the edge of the salad. Sprinkle with cress. Serve salad dressing separately so guests can toss their own salad.

Hearty Bacon Scones

1 cup whole wheat flour

1 cup all-purpose flour

1 tablespoon baking powder

3/4 teaspoon salt

1/3 cup margarine

1/2 cup crumbled, cooked bacon

3/4 cup milk

ε•Preheat oven to 450F. Combine first four ingredients in a bowl. Cut in margarine until mixture is crumbly. Mix in the bacon. Gradually add enough milk to form a soft dough. Turn out onto a floured board and kneed just until dough is no longer sticky. Roll out to about 1/2-inch thick. Cut into rounds with a 2-inch cookie cutter. Place on an ungreased baking sheet. Brush tops with milk. Bake for about 15 minutes or until well risen and browned. Cool for ten minutes on a wire rack. Serve fresh with salad.

Yorkshire Apple Tart

❧ Preheat oven to 375F. Lightly grease an 8-inch tart pan. Break off 1/3 of pastry dough. On a floured board, roll out larger piece of pastry and line tart pan. Peel, core and slice apples. Arrange slices in pastry shell. Sprinkle with water and sugar. Roll out remaining pastry and use to cover the tart. Lightly seal edges. Brush with milk and sprinkle with sugar. Bake for 20 to 25 minutes or until crust is firm and lightly browned. Cool for 15 minutes on a wire rack. With the tip of a sharp knife, gently break the seal on the crust and remove the top. Cover apples with sliced cheese. Replace top. Return to oven for a further 15 minutes. Serve warm.

2-1/2 cup quantity pie pastry
3/4 lb. baking apples
2 tablespoons sugar
1 tablespoon water
milk and sugar to glaze
1/4 lb. mature Cheddar cheese, sliced

Date Bars

❧ Preheat oven to 350F. Lightly grease a 7-inch square cake pan. Sift flour and combine with oatmeal. Cut in butter until mixture is like fine breadcrumbs. Divide in two, and press one half in the bottom of the cake pan. Set aside remainder. Combine dates and water in a saucepan and bring to a boil. Simmer until very soft, remove from heat and allow to cool. Stir in lemon juice, honey and cinnamon. Spread evenly over dough in cake pan. Cover with remaining dough. Bake for about 25 minutes. Remove from oven and cut into 12 bars. Cool in pan on a wire rack. When cold, re-cut bars and present on a serving platter.

1 cup all-purpose flour
1-3/4 cups oatmeal
1 cup butter
1-1/4 cups pitted dates, chopped
2 tablespoons water
1 tablespoon lemon juice
1 tablespoon honey
1/4 teaspoon cinnamon

Suspended Grapes

2 packages lime gelatine
    dessert
1 bunch green grapes
Whipped cream

🍇 Make up one package of dessert as directed. Pour into a large, attractive glass bowl. Chill until firm. Wash grapes and pat dry, being careful to keep all grapes attached to the bunch. Arrange grapes attractively on top of gelatin dessert. Make up second package of dessert. Allow to cool but not set. Gently pour over grapes. Chill until firm. The bunch of grapes will appear "suspended" in jelly. Serve with whipped cream.

Literary Tea Salon

The upper echelons of Victorian society were great patrons of the arts, and had lofty intellectual affectations. They gathered in each other's homes at teatime for "musicales," book readings and lectures. Percy Bysshe Shelley is quoted as saying, "Teas, where small talk dies in agonies." But that hardly seems the case. As proof, read this item from the society pages of a Philadelphia newspaper in 1893.

"Mrs. John Sherwood, that interesting and indefatigable old lady, is giving a series of lectures on fashionable subjects in the most elegant parlors of the city. She gathers the cream of the *beau monde* about her. Mrs. Sherwood thoroughly understands her listeners. They want the *cafe frappe'* of ideas on all subjects, and she give them just what they ask for, beaten very light and frothy indeed.

"In contrast to the charming whipped cream of Mrs. Sherwood are the intense, original dramatic lectures of Mrs. Florence Williams. She dissects Balzac with the keenest knife of criticism, and takes one into the innermost darkness of Dantean imagination. She has the head and deep tones of a man. She stirs one's interest and makes one think. Her audiences are not as large as Mrs. Sherwood's, but they are made up of cleverer people."

Your own salon need not be nearly so pretentious. Consider meeting with a group of friends on a regular basis, perhaps rotating homes, to informally discuss current books, films and music. Enjoy the company, gossip a little, and of course, have a great tea.

Menu for Ten

Open-faced Roquefort Sandwiches

Pikelets

Featherweight Chocolate Sponge

Sesame Seed Cookies

Figs with Cream

Victoria's Treasure Earl Grey Tea

Open-faced Roquefort Sandwiches

1/2 lb. Roquefort cheese, room temperature

4 tablespoons unsalted butter, diced

Pinch of cayenne pepper to taste

3 tablespoons brandy

10 slices fresh white bread

ॐ Crumble the cheese. Put cheese and butter in a food processor or blender and process until creamy. Season with cayenne. Beat in brandy. Lightly toast the bread. Cut off crusts. Spread toast with cheese mixture and cut each slice diagonally into four triangles.

Pikelets

1/2 cup milk

1 teaspoon white vinegar

1 cup all-purpose flour

1 teaspoon baking powder

1/4 teaspoon baking soda

Pinch of salt

3 tablespoons sugar

1 egg lightly beaten

1 tablespoon butter, melted

2 tablespoons golden raisins

ॐ Combine milk and vinegar and set aside for 5 minutes. Preheat a griddle or heavy skillet over medium heat. Sift flour, baking powder, baking soda and salt. Add sugar. Mix in milk, egg and butter. Stir in raisins. Spray griddle or skillet with cooking spray. Drop heaping tablespoonfuls of batter onto griddle. Cook about two minutes or until undersides are brown and bubbles form on top. Flip over and cook other side for 2 minutes. Serve warm with butter.

Featherweight
Chocolate Sponge

Preheat oven to 350F. Lightly grease an 8-inch round cake pan. Line with wax paper and grease again. Dust lightly with flour. In a small saucepan, heat sugar and water to boiling. Cover and simmer for 5 minutes. Strain and set aside to cool. Sift flour, cocoa, baking powder and salt together. Set aside. Separate eggs. Combine all 4 egg whites with lemon juice and beat until foamy. While beating, pour 1/3 cup syrup into egg whites and continue beating until a soft meringue forms. Cover and set aside. Mix together 2 egg yolks, vanilla, butter and remaining syrup. Add dry ingredients to egg yolk mixture. Add meringue and gently mix into a smooth batter. Pour into the cake pan. Bake for 25 minutes or until a wooden pick inserted in the center comes out clean. Cool in pan for 10 minutes. Transfer to a wire rack to cool completely. Arrange on a doily covered cake plate. For a more substantial cake, make a double mixture and cook in two pans. When cool, sandwich together with Victoria's Treasure Raspberry Jam and dust top with powdered sugar.

1/2 cup sugar

1/4 cup water

3/4 cup cake flour

1/3 cup unsweetened cocoa

1 1/4 teaspoons baking powder

Pinch of salt

2 eggs plus 2 whites

1/4 teaspoon lemon juice

1/2 teaspoon vanilla

1/4 cup unsalted butter, melted

Sesame Seed Cookies

1/4 cup plus 3 tablespoons
  light olive oil

1/2 tablespoon aniseed

1/2 tablespoon sesame
  seeds

1/2 cup plus 1 tablespoon
  sugar

1/4 cup lemon juice

1/2 teaspoon grated lemon
  peel

1/2 teaspoon grated
  orange peel

2 1/4 cups all-purpose
  flour

1 tablespoon cinnamon

🍂 Preheat oven t 375F. In a saucepan, heat oil, aniseed and sesame seeds over a medium heat for 5 minutes. Cool, then add 1/2 cup sugar, lemon juice, lemon peel and orange peel. Combine flour and 1/2 tablespoon cinnamon. Gradually stir dry ingredients into oil mixture. Cover and set aside for 30 minutes. On a lightly floured board, roll out dough to a thickness of 1/4 inch. Cut into rounds with a 2-inch cookie cutter. Place on an ungreased baking sheet and bake for 12 to 15 minutes or until light golden brown. Combine remaining sugar and cinnamon and sprinkle over hot cookies. Transfer to wire racks and cool completely.

Figs with Cream

10 ripe purple figs

3/4 cup heavy cream

1 1/2 tablespoons sugar

1 teaspoon Grand Marnier

2 tablespoons finely
  chopped pecans

🍂 With a sharp knife, cut the stems from the figs. Starting at the narrow end, cut each fig into quarters stopping 1/4-inch from the bottom. Arrange the figs on the serving platter and gently spread them open as far as possible without breaking them apart. Whip the cream until it starts to thicken. Beat in sugar and continue whipping until soft peaks form. Beat in Grand Marnier. Spoon a dollop of whipped cream in the center of each fig. Sprinkle with nuts.

Index

Source Directory

Victoria's Treasure teas, preserves and honey are available from the following stores. Many of these sources also carry other gourmet specialties that will be make your tea party authentic and delicious. Should you live in an area not listed, Victoria's Treasure teas are available by mail order directly from the company.

Barnie's
340 North Primrose Drive
Orlando, Fl 32803
(407) 894-1416

Bernard's Coffees of the World
950 North Star Mall
San Antonio, TX 78216
(512) 344-2906

The Brewery
249 Santa Monica Place
Santa Monica, CA 90401
(213) 393-7793

Candyman
2446 Beacon Avenue
Sidney, BC
Canada V8L 1X6
(604) 656-1333

Capt. Bean's
7426 S.E. 36
Portland, OR 97202
(503) 652-2389

Cestino Bello
30211 Golden Lantern, #A
Laguna Niguel, CA 92677
(714) 363-9905

Coffee Ole'
1644 Hillside Avenue
Hillside Shopping Center
Victoria, BC
Canada V8T 2C5
(604) 595-2739

Cookery N'Orleans Style
812 Decatur Street
New Orleans, LA 70116
(504) 561-8482

Golden Pheasant Coffee & Tea
Crossroads Mall, #136
Boulder, C 80301
(303) 440-4464

Gloria Jeans
1064 Town Center Lane
Sunnyvale, CA 94086
(408) 720-1871

Gloria Jeans
Galleria Mall
5085 West Heimer Road
Houston, TX 77056
(713) 623-8055

Joffrey's
4517 West Ohio
Tampa, FL 33614
(813) 251-3315

Kitchen Kitchen
74-921 Highway 111
Indian Wells, CA 92210
(619) 773-9464

Market Spice
2747 152nd Avenue, N.E.
Redmond, WA 98502
(206) 883-1220

Sparrow Hawk
12 E. Bijou (downtown)
Colorado Springs, CO 80903
(719) 471-3235

Swiss Colony
7200 W. Alameda Avenue
Villaitalia Mall Upper Level
Lakewood, CO 80226
(303) 936-8140

Tradewinds Spice
6507 W. North Avenue
Wauwatosa, WI 53513
(414) 257-3368

Vices & Spices
3558 State Street
Santa Barbara, CA 93105
(805) 687-7196

Victoria's Treasure
Tea 2000
9926 Pioneer Boulevard, # 101
& 102
Santa Fe Springs, CA 90670
(800) 4488-TEA

TEA OF THE MONTH CLUB ™

Victoria's Treasure is a line of award-winning, gourmet Indian teas including classic Darjeeling, full-bodied Assam, aromatic Nilgiri, and blends such as Earl Grey and English Breakfast. We also have an extensive array of Ceylon teas blended with natural fruit oils and exotic spices — everything from mandarin to peach, from blackberry to mango, pineapple, cardamom, ginger, vanilla and brandy.

Apart from the excellent quality of tea, what distinguishes Victoria's Treasure from others is its distinctive packaging. Loose tea comes in small wooden chests, brass caddies, velvet pouches and a unique hand made terra cotta pot decorated in an Indian motif.

Now this superlative tea is available to you by mail order through TEA OF THE MONTH CLUB ™. Once a member you will receive not only a regular sampling of our teas but also a newsletter and special offers for the tea connoisseur. For further information call 1-800-4488-TEA or send in the coupon below.

PLEASE SEND TEA OF THE MONTH CLUB ™ INFORMATION

Name _____

Address _____

City _____

State_____ ZIP _____

Tea 2000, 9926 Pioneer Blvd, Towers 101 & 102,
Santa Fe Springs, CA 90670

ORDER FORM

To order additional copies of "A Victorian Teatime Treasury," simply fill out the attached coupon. The book makes a perfect gift for the tea lover as well as those who like to entertain or are fans of Victoriana.

And if you enjoyed this book, you might want to order:

- "The Pleasures of Afternoon Tea," hardcover, 160 pages, 60 color photographs, 150 traditional English recipes.

- "Low Calorie Teatime Treats," paperback, 104 pages, black and white illustrations, your favorite tea recipes reduced in fat and calorie content.

Quantity   Total

_____ A Victorian Teatime Treasury $ 9.95   _____

_____ The Pleasure of Afternoon Tea $19.95   _____

_____ Low Calorie Teatime Treats $ 9.95   _____

California residents add 6.5% sales tax   _____

Shipping and Handling for first book   ___$2.00___

$1.00 for each additional book   _____

Total Enclosed   _____

Name _____

Address _____

City _____

State_____ ZIP _____

Tea 2000, 9926 Pioneer Blvd, Towers 101 & 102,
Santa Fe Springs, CA 90670

ABOUT THE AUTHOR

Angela Hynes, author of "A Victorian Teatime Treasury," is a native of Manchester, England who has now lived in Santa Monica, California for ten years. A former caterer turned writer, her work has appeared in *Family Circle, Woman's Day, Cook's Magazine, Lear's, Longevity, Playgirl, Los Angeles Magazine,* and many other national and local publications. She has also been an editor at *Slimmer* and *Moxie* magazines. "A Victorian Teatime Treasury," is Hynes' fifth book and a fitting follow-up to "The Pleasures of Afternoon Tea," her best-selling and highly reviewed book on the history, romance, etiquette and recipes of this noble, English tradition. The book is now in its sixth printing.

Hynes has appeared on numerous television and radio talk shows and is in demand as a public speaker. She also does cooking demonstrations of afternoon tea recipes, often in conjunction with Victoria's Treasure Teas, for whom she is national spokesperson.